As one of the world's longest established
and best-known travel brands,
Thomas Cook are the experts in travel.

For more than 135 years our
guidebooks have unlocked the secrets
of destinations around the world,
sharing with travellers a wealth of
experience and a passion for travel.

**Rely on Thomas Cook as your
travelling companion on your next trip
and benefit from our unique heritage.**

Thomas Cook **pocket** guides

LINCOLN

Your travelling companion since 1873

Thomas
Cook

Written by David Cawley

Published by Thomas Cook Publishing
A division of Thomas Cook Tour Operations Limited
Company registration no. 3772199 England
The Thomas Cook Business Park, Unit 9, Coningsby Road,
Peterborough PE3 8SB, United Kingdom
Email: books@thomascook.com, Tel: +44 (0) 1733 416477
www.thomascookpublishing.com

Produced by Cambridge Publishing Management Limited
Burr Elm Court, Main Street, Caldecote CB23 7NU
www.cambridgepm.co.uk

ISBN: 978-1-84848-498-6

This first edition © 2011 Thomas Cook Publishing
Text © Thomas Cook Publishing
Cartography supplied by Redmoor Design, Tavistock, Devon
Map data © OpenStreetMap contributors CC-BY-SA, www.openstreetmap.org,
http://creativecommons.org

Series Editor: Karen Beaulah
Production/DTP: Steven Collins

Printed and bound in Spain by GraphyCems

Cover photography © Brian Lawrence

CONTENTS

INTRODUCING LINCOLN

Introduction...............................6

When to go 8

History.....................................10

Culture....................................12

MAKING THE MOST OF LINCOLN

Shopping.................................14

Eating & drinking 16

Entertainment.........................18

Sport & relaxation...................20

Accommodation 22

The best of Lincoln 26

Suggested itineraries 28

Something for nothing.........30

When it rains............................31

On arrival..................................32

THE CITY OF LINCOLN

Introduction to city areas 42

City North,
    the Uphill district................44

City South,
    the Downhill district..........66

OUT OF TOWN TRIPS

Lincolnshire Wolds 80

Skegness 84

Sleaford...................................86

PRACTICAL INFORMATION

Directory..................................90

INDEX 94

MAPS

Lincoln.....................................34

Lincoln city centre 43

Lincoln region 81

SYMBOLS KEY

The following symbols are used throughout this book:

ⓐ address ❶ telephone ⓦ website address ⓔ email
ⓛ opening times ⓝ public transport connections ❶ important

The following symbols are used on the maps:

🅸 information office	▦	point of interest
✉ post office	O	city
🛡 police station	O	large town
🚌 bus station	○	small town
🚆 railway station	═	motorway
🅿🚌 park & ride	▬	main road
✝ cathedral		minor road
🛍 shopping	—	railway
❶ numbers denote featured cafés, restaurants & venues		

PRICE CATEGORIES

The ratings below indicate average price rates for a double
room per night, including breakfast:

£ under £70 ££ £70–100 £££ over £100

The typical cost for a three-course meal without drinks
is as follows:

£ under £20 ££ £20–30 £££ over £30

ⓞ Lincoln's famous cathedral

INTRODUCING
Lincoln

Introduction

Lincoln is an enthralling city, a place of great charm, history and style, all set in some of England's greenest and most pleasant countryside. Located high above the plains of Lincolnshire, in eastern central England, Lincoln is the region's principal city and has been a place of pilgrimage, trade and courtly goings-on for over 2,000 years. Much of this heritage remains, but Lincoln hasn't stood still, and its story today is very much one of two cities, a place with two highly distinct personalities.

In the Uphill district to the north, the cathedral crowns the city like a beacon. A soaring structure dating from the 12th century, Lincoln Cathedral is one of the finest Gothic buildings in Europe, and every bit as magnificent as the famed cathedrals of York, Durham, Canterbury and Salisbury. The castle nearby and the cobbled streets lined with picturesque medieval buildings are a delight not only for those enthralled by history but also for shoppers and foodies.

The Downhill district, comprising the modern city centre, is Lincoln's other face. Though not as aesthetically enticing as the Uphill district, this area offers attractions of a different kind, especially for those who enjoy a vibrant city nightlife.

Despite all this and more, Lincoln is – astonishingly – still off the main tourist radar. In a recent survey, when asked what they most closely associated with the city, 87 per cent of respondents named Lincoln's famous sausage rather than any of its major historic attractions! Much to the bafflement of local people, Lincoln has always had trouble joining the heady ranks of England's other more famous cities. It is true that it narrowly falls short of the 'hidden gem' category, but the obvious benefit for visitors is that, aside from the shuffling Yuletide crush during its famous Christmas Market, Lincoln's streets and attractions remain relatively tranquil by comparison to those of other cities.

Lincoln's location, slightly off the beaten track in relation to Britain's main transport networks, may partly explain why it attracts fewer visitors than other British cities. But the small amount of extra time and trouble involved in getting there only adds to its allure: Lincoln is truly worthy of the effort.

◆ Detail on the Guildhall

When to go

SEASONS & CLIMATE

If you can forgive the notoriously unpredictable weather endured by the British and come prepared for its foibles, then there is never really a bad time to visit this part of the UK. Influenced by close proximity to the eastern coastline of the North Sea, spring and summer are undoubtedly the seasons when the city is at its most climatically affable. The sun makes more regular appearances, temperatures reach averages of 20°C (68°F) to 21°C (70°F), flowers burst into bloom and in the evening the city's streets fill with the buzz of alfresco eating and drinking. From November to March rainfall increases, and temperatures drop to between 2°C (36°F) and 7°C (45°F). As April approaches, the mercury begins to rise again and average precipitation levels fall. In accordance with British Summer Time (BST), clocks go forward an hour on the last Sunday of March and back one hour on the last Sunday of October, when they revert to Greenwich Mean Time (GMT).

ANNUAL EVENTS

All year round in Lincoln, the seasons are punctuated by a diverse and plentiful succession of events. The summer season kicks off in the third week of June with the agriculture-themed **Lincolnshire Show** (Ⓦ www.lincolnshireshow.info). This is followed by the **Lincoln Waterfront Festival**, a free family entertainment-fest in July, and by the embracing of all things Italia during the **Italian Weekend**. During the last weekends of

July and September Lincoln's regular, and highly popular, **Artist Markets** take over the streets along The Strait.

August is a busy month, with the **Lincolnshire International Chamber Music Festival** (w www.licmf.org.uk), the annual celebration of things gay, lesbian, bisexual and trans-life at **Lincoln Pride** (w www.lincolnpride.co.uk), and the **BIG Art Event**, when artists head to Brayford Pool to display their works. In September, history enthusiasts will enjoy the free admissions to Lincoln's historic buildings during the city's **Heritage Open Days** (w www.heritageopendays.org.uk).

At the beginning of October, smash comedic talent can be enjoyed at the city's **Comedy Festival** (w www.lincolncomedy festival.co.uk). Finally, the beginning of December sees the enormously popular festive sights, sounds and smells of **Lincoln Christmas Market** (w http://lincoln-christmasmarket.co.uk). For further details, see page 93.

○ *Autumnal sunshine in Minster Yard*

History

You only need to look at Lincoln's geographical setting to understand why it was coveted by a long succession of conquerors. Perched high on a solitary hill with a commanding view of the surrounding flatlands, it was overrun by the conquering Roman Ninth Hispanic Legion in AD 48. The Romans were drawn to the defensive advantages of the site's elevation. The fact that it had a potential inland harbour connected to the sea by the river running at the foot of the hill made it clear to those matter-of-fact and ever-efficient Romans that the place should be named Lindum (later Lindum Colonia), or 'Fort by the Pool'.

A city was born, and over the following centuries it was to become a significant centre of imperial trade, facilitated not only by ships sailing in and out of what is now known as

● *Pottergate, whose name dates back to the Vikings*

Brayford Pool, but by road along the superhighways of the day: the Fosse Way to Exeter to the southwest, and Ermine Street, which passed through the city centre and northwards on to York and southwards to London (today the A1 and A15 follow much of its route). Following the Roman withdrawal in the 5th century, the next to take control of the city arrived from Scandinavia. They were the Vikings, who, once they tired of vandalism and pillaging, continued to see their newly acquired city flourish. In 1068, the Normans under William the Conqueror arrived and immediately set to work building the castle and the grandiose masterpiece of Lincoln Cathedral.

Through the following centuries Lincoln prospered as a busy centre of the cloth and wool trade. However, in the 19th century engineering became the mainstay of the local economy, with the city becoming especially renowned for its engines, tanks and aircraft production. In more recent times, heavy industry has given way to the service industries, with IT, retail, education and tourism now underpinning Lincoln's economy.

VIKING STREET NAMES

For first-time visitors the names of some of Lincoln's thoroughfares may seem a little confusing, if not intriguing. Street names in the oldest parts of the city include Pottergate, Saltergate and Bailgate. The suffix 'gate' in these names is derived from *gata*, the Viking word for 'street'. These ancient names give a clue as to the original function, trades or destination of Lincoln's historic streets.

Culture

If Lincoln has an ace up its sleeve, it is a strong sense of heritage fuelled by a progressive attitude to culture, so those in search of enlightenment will find plenty to keep them engaged during their visit. **Lincoln Cathedral** is a magnificent demonstration of medieval craft and dedication, while the neighbouring **Medieval Bishops' Palace** is one of the finest of its kind in England. Within the 900-year-old walls of **Lincoln Castle** is an intriguing group of buildings that contain one of only four copies of **Magna Carta**. **The Collection** is a modern showcase for local archaeological and historical artefacts dating from the Iron Age through to the Middle Ages. The **Museum of Lincolnshire Life** documents more recent history, including the daily lives of its humbler populace and the significant role that Lincoln played during World War II. Anyone with even a passing interest in art should head to both The **Usher Gallery** and the smaller **Sam Scorer Gallery**. All these attractions are located in the Uphill district.

● *Castle Square is a good place to rest your feet*

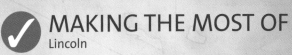

MAKING THE MOST OF
Lincoln

Shopping

Pure indulgence for shoppers, Lincoln serves up size and variety in two very distinct areas. Located in the captivating Uphill district, particularly along Bailgate and the cobbled Steep Hill and The Strait, is a cornucopia of high-quality independent shops all housed in beautifully preserved historic buildings.

Below the concentrated cluster of these ancient streets, the city takes on a completely different personality. This is the modern face of Lincoln's retail magnetism, fronted by a long parade of household favourites that stretch along the High Street and surrounding thoroughfares. The **Waterside Shopping Centre** includes over 30 predominantly fashion outlets over three levels, with a small food court on the top level. **St Mark's Shopping Centre**, housed in a converted railway station, accommodates an array of major flagship stores that continue south along Tritton Road. There are also several fast- food restaurants here in which to take a breather.

Traditional markets, both regular and seasonal, also play a big part in the city's commercial fabric. Cornhill and Central Market Halls, west of the High Street, are filled with cheery stalls selling everything from bargain basics to treats and small luxuries. Regular street markets are also held throughout the year. These include the Lincoln Craft Fair around Cornhill (🕒 09.00–16.00 Sat) and the farmers' markets on Castle Square (🕒 09.00–16.00 first Fri of the month), City Square (🕒 09.00–16.00 third Sat of the month) and the High Street (🕒 09.00–16.00 second Wed of the month). The city's most exciting market is undoubtedly its four-day Christmas Market (see page 9). This essentially German market is almost too popular at peak times, and it can be difficult to negotiate a path through the crowds, but it still remains a uniquely magical retail event.

◆ Bailgate has many independent shops

Eating & drinking

When it comes to satisfying hunger and slaking thirst Lincoln covers just about all the bases from fine dining to gastropubs, most of which offer good local ales (try Batemans, the local brew) and global menus. Cafés and delis are plentiful and offer a selection of goodies for a picnic, perhaps to be enjoyed around Brayford Pool, beside the River Witham (by City Square) or surrounded by the greenery of the Arboretum or Temple Gardens.

But this is only part of the story. In Lincolnshire, food is almost revered. It is a key part of the local economy. The region's rich, fertile soil is hugely important for growing local produce; in fact Lincolnshire is Britain's principal source of cereal, wheat, potatoes, brassicas and peas. Ultimately, this verdant land also contributes to the creation of some very fine cheeses, such as the soft veined Cote Hill Blue, the Edam-like Cote Hill Yellow (known locally as 'Yellow Belly') and the well-matured Lincolnshire Poacher. The last is often served grilled over another traditional local favourite, the moist and fruity plum loaf.

Lesser known, and much tastier than they sound, are Lincolnshire haslet (loaf of pigs' offal) and stuffed chine, a cheap cut of pork traditionally stuffed with parsley, boiled then sliced and served cold. Lincolnshire's famous herb-rich sausages are soon to share the same protected-name status as champagne or Parma ham. Such is the esteem in which the humble banger is held that it even has its own festival, on the last weekend of October. Look out for the Taste of Lincolnshire signs, which confirm that the establishment has met guidelines on provenance and quality, and overall dedication to the produce of Lincolnshire's soil and sea.

◬ *There are plenty of places to eat by the river*

Entertainment

In terms of its nightlife, all that Lincoln has to offer can be clearly divided into two distinct categories. Evening revelry in the Downhill district moves along at a fair, sometimes raucous pace, especially in the modern venues, clubs and contemporary bars on and around the university campus. Those who prefer their social drinking without the pounding bass beats will appreciate the cordiality of the traditional, and in some cases seriously old, hostelries in the Uphill district. This is also, incidentally, the realm of spirits of the dark side, which are conjured up in a number of regular ghost walks through the city's spooky past (see page 65).

HOLLY HOOD

As well as Lincoln's featuring in *The Da Vinci Code*, *Young Victoria* and *Oliver Twist*, the wool trade that made the city so prosperous also gave it a bit part in the global folklore of **Robin Hood**. In the legend, the tunic worn by the 12th-century hero is described as being made of cloth dyed a colour known as Lincoln Green. Since its first screen appearance in 1908, this hue has clothed Hollywood actors including Douglas Fairbanks, Errol Flynn, Kevin Costner, an animated fox and Russell Crowe. No definitive agreement has been reached as to Lincoln Green's exact shade, and authorities on the subject even suggest that it also came in white, grey and scarlet.

Fans of the silver screen can enjoy both the latest blockbusters and more artistic releases in a choice of two venues (see pages 72 & 54). Theatre is represented by both traditional touring productions and more challenging works (see pages 53, 54 & 72), while during the day street performers often demonstrate their various, and varying, talents on Castle Square and along the High Street. Details of all forms of entertainment can be obtained from the Visitor Information Centre and from the free student publication *The Linc* (see page 93). *The Lincolnshire Echo*, the local newspaper, also carries listings.

🔺 *The Shed is popular with LU students*

Sport & relaxation

Although it isn't exactly big on spectator sports, Lincoln still has two professional football teams. Lincoln City FC, nicknamed 'The Imps' (see page 54), languishes in the lower leagues but it does offer a fix for fans of the beautiful game (ⓐ Sincil Bank Stadium ① 01522 880011 ⓦ www.redimps.co.uk ⓝ Bus: 1, 7, 13, 14, plus a short walk ① Admission charge). The city is also home to a professional women's football team, Lincoln City LFC (ⓦ www.lincolnladiesfc.co.uk).

Fans of horse racing should head to Market Rasen (ⓐ Legsby Road, Market Rasen ① 0844 579 3009 ⓦ www.marketrasenraces.co.uk ① Admission charge). Golf enthusiasts are spoilt for choice: Lincolnshire has no fewer than 56 courses, including Canwick Park (ⓐ Washingborough Road ① 01522 542912 ⓦ www.canwickpark.org) and the National Golf Centre at Woodhall Spa (ⓐ The Broadway, Woodhall Spa ① 01526 352511 ⓦ www.woodhallspagolf.com).

For more gentle pursuits, make for the rolling hills of the Lincolnshire Wolds or Lincolnshire's coastline, both of which are ideal for some gentle walking. Visit Lincolnshire has a collection of route 'Discovery Packs' (see page 93). Lincolnshire's quiet lanes and off-road trails also make it a haven for cyclists. Route maps are downloadable (see page 40) or obtainable at the Visitor Information Centre (see page 93).

For the simple pleasures of enjoying some greenery and birdsong away from urban bustle, seek out the Arboretum and Temple Gardens. Also, just beyond the city limits are the nature trails and lakes of Hartsholme Country Park (ⓐ Skellingthorpe

Road ✆ 01522 873577 ⓦ www.hartsholmecountrypark.com
🕐 24 hours (Visitor centre 09.00–17.00 daily (summer); 09.00–
16.00 daily (winter) Ⓝ Bus: 66) and Whisby Nature Park (ⓐ Moor
Lane, Thorpe on the Hill ✆ 01522 688868 ⓦ www.natural
worldcentre.co.uk 🕐 09.00–17.00 daily (summer); 09.00–16.30
daily (winter) Ⓝ Bus: 46).

⬤ The Arboretum is just a short walk from the city centre

Accommodation

Lincoln offers a comprehensive choice of corporate and independent hotels as well as a selection of homely B&Bs and rural campsites and caravan sites. Availability is generally no problem, except perhaps in December during the Christmas Market (see page 9), when hotels may be booked up. Another peak time is late September, when the arrival of new university students and their accompanying parents may also have an impact on the availability of hotel accommodation. At either of these times, it is wise to book a room in advance. If you arrive at short notice, the Visitor Information Centre (see page 93) on Castle Hill will be happy to find you a room for the night.

HOTELS

Ibis Hotel £ This modern budget hotel is about 8 km (5 miles) south of the city centre yet easily accessible by road. It has free parking, a bar and a café. Wi-Fi (❶ Charge) is available throughout its contemporary and well-equipped rooms.
ⓐ Runcorn Road, off Whisby Road ❶ 01522 698333
ⓦ www.ibishotel.com

Holiday Inn ££ Situated in the Downhill district, overlooking Brayford Pool and the university, and within a short walk of Lincoln's shopping and business district, this wharf-style building houses a mini-gym along with all the usual refinements, including an attractive waterside terrace.
ⓐ Brayford Wharf North ❶ 01522 544244 ⓦ www.holiday inn.com

The Lincoln Hotel ££ Behind its rather unbeguiling frontage, The Lincoln reveals itself as a modern hotel furnished in bright, retro style. It is located in the historic Uphill district, so that most of its public areas offer fine vistas across to the neighbouring cathedral; it's worth asking for a room with the same outlook. Its location also makes it ideal for sightseeing. **ⓐ** Eastgate **ⓣ** 01522 520348 **ⓦ** www.thelincolnhotel.com

Washingborough Hall ££ Guests can enjoy relaxed yet not over-expensive splendour at this country house hotel set in its own private grounds. Only 5 km (3 miles) from the city centre, many of this Georgian building's period features have been retained and incorporate 21st-century facilities. **ⓐ** Church Hill, Washingborough **ⓣ** 01522 790340 **ⓦ** www.washingboroughhall.com

The White Hart Hotel ££ In this hotel at the core of the city's historic Uphill district, the public areas are slick and smart and, as in the bedrooms, old-world charm blends with 21st-century style and technology. Endeavour to secure a room with a view of the cathedral. **ⓐ** Bailgate **ⓣ** 01522 526222 **ⓦ** www.whitehart-lincoln.co.uk

Charlotte House £££ Highly regarded, award-winning 5-star hotel sympathetically created from the remnants of a former hospital complex. Set in its own tranquil grounds in the shadow of the castle walls, it is just a short stroll from the city's historic sites. The rooms have original period features but are also equipped with the latest in gadgetry, including

free Wi-Fi. ⓐ The Lawns, Union Road ⓣ 01522 541000
ⓦ www.charlottehouselincoln.com

GUESTHOUSES

The Old Bakery £ Located in the Uphill district, this restaurant offers guesthouse accommodation in a small number of simply furnished, bijou rooms. Wi-Fi is available throughout. The restaurant (see page 64) is one of the city's most celebrated establishments. ⓐ 26–28 Burton Road ⓣ 01522 576057
ⓦ www.theold-bakery.co.uk

The Old Rectory £ This large Victorian house is located in a quiet street of the Uphill district just a few minutes' walk from the city's main historic attractions. Although its rooms are a little plain, it offers good value for money and a friendly welcome. There is also a private car park. ⓐ 19 Newport ⓣ 01522 514774
ⓦ www.theoldrectorylincoln.co.uk

Bailhouse Hotel ££ Few centrally located hotels in Lincoln can boast a heated swimming pool, as this one does. Situated in the Uphill district, this historic and lovingly restored ten-bedroom town house offers a wealth of old-world charm. Self-catering is also available. ⓐ 34 Bailgate ⓣ 01522 541000
ⓦ http://bailhouse.co.uk

SELF-CATERING

The Crown Windmill ££ This 19th-century converted windmill in the Downhill district offers an unusual self-catering option. There are four lovingly decorated bedrooms, as well as a lounge, dining room and kitchen, and a pool room on the top level. ⓐ Princess Street ⓣ 01522 533562 ⓦ www.thecrown windmill.co.uk ⓘ Minimum two-night stay and limited internal access for those with mobility problems. No stag or hen parties

Lincoln Holiday Homes ££ These are peaceful rural chalets and barn conversions scattered around the outskirts of the city. They can be reached either on foot or on the bicycles that are provided for guests. The homes are well presented and well equipped with modern comforts, and come in a variety of sizes. ⓐ Fen Farm, Skellingthorpe Road and Riseholme House, Riseholme ⓣ 07774 112990 ⓦ www.lincolnholidayhomes.co.uk

CAMPING & CARAVANING

Hartsholme Country Park £ Tents, caravans and motorhomes are all welcome at this site, which is not the closest to Lincoln though it is set in picturesque surroundings (see pages 20–21). ⓣ 01522 873578

Willow Holt £ Close to Tattershall, Coningsby and Woodhall Spa, this large site is 45 minutes by road from Lincoln and accommodates tents, caravans and motorhomes. ⓐ Lodge Road, Tattershall ⓣ 01526 343111 ⓦ www.willowholt.co.uk ⓝ Bus: 5, plus a 25-minute walk

THE BEST OF LINCOLN

Demure in size, big in charm and history, Lincoln offers an enthralling range of things to do and see, not only in the city itself but also in the attractive countryside all around and eastwards to the coast.

TOP 10 ATTRACTIONS

- **Lincoln Castle** Commanding magnificent views, the castle also contains fascinating exhibits from its days as a prison (see page 47).

- **Lincoln Cathedral** One of the finest Gothic buildings in Europe, this is a 'must-see' on any visit to the city (see page 49).

- **Christmas Market** This German-style market creates a magical atmosphere, radiating the warmth of the festive season (see page 9).

- **The Collection** This new space traces the city's long history, with a particular focus on its very early years (see page 53).

- **City Ghost Walks** An evening stroll around old Lincoln reveals ghoulish tales of skulduggery and the paranormal (see page 65).

- **Lincolnshire Wolds** This bucolic scenery is criss-crossed by walking and cycling trails between picturesque towns and villages (see page 80).

- **Medieval streets** Lincoln's enchanting ancient streets are alive with interesting shops and enticing restaurants (see page 52).

- **Museum of Lincolnshire Life** Documenting local heritage, the museum places special emphasis on the past 300 years (see page 55).

- **Skegness** Seaside fun, sandy beaches and tranquil nature reserves can be enjoyed at this famous resort (see page 84).

- **Usher Gallery** Lincoln's primary art space hosts touring and permanent exhibitions of traditional and contemporary art (see page 56).

🔻 *The Norman House on Steep Hill*

Suggested itineraries

HALF-DAY: LINCOLN IN A HURRY

If time is against you, head straight for Lincoln's Uphill district to explore the cathedral and the castle, perhaps stopping to grab a quick coffee in one of the choice cafés or pubs that cluster between the two.

1 DAY: TIME TO SEE A LITTLE MORE

Again the Uphill district should be the focus for a day's stay, and some more leisurely sightseeing. After exploring the castle and the cathedral, take a deep breath and amble up and down the cobbled Steep Hill and The Strait. The historic houses now contain tempting independent shops and cafés. Stop for lunch here to sample local specialities and rest weary legs.

2–3 DAYS: SHORT CITY-BREAK

A few days to spend in Lincoln will give you enough time to do the city justice. All within the Uphill district and within easy reach of each other are the Museum of Lincolnshire Life, the Medieval Bishops' Palace, The Collection and the Usher Gallery. For some verdant peace and fine views over the city and landscapes beyond, head to the Arboretum or Temple Gardens, or make for the hidden botanic gems at the neighbouring Joseph Banks Conservatory and John Dawber Garden. There is plenty of time to make the most of the Downhill district too, perhaps taking a cruise along the Fossdyke from Brayford Pool and indulging in some shopping in the city's concentration of big-name stores.

LONGER: ENJOYING LINCOLN TO THE FULL

With even more time at your disposal, you can head beyond the city limits and into the delights that the county of Lincolnshire has to offer. To the north are the Lincolnshire Wolds, gentle pastureland dotted with towns and villages. It's ideal for some easy cycling and gentle walking. To the east is the coast, where on the one hand is Skegness, with its garish, uninhibited fun and sandy beaches, and on the other the tranquil, protected landscapes of Gibraltar Point. To the south lies more rich farmland liberally peppered with attractive small settlements and a collection of operational and historic airfields now dedicated to evocative accounts of World War II aviation.

🔺 A Lancaster bomber at the Lincolnshire Aviation Heritage Centre

Something for nothing

Thankfully, the Museum of Lincolnshire Life, the Usher Gallery and The Collection are already refreshingly free to enter. The historic streets all around them in the Uphill district offer the simple and enthralling pleasures of ambling exploration, aided by a series of enlightening information boards that outline the history of noteworthy buildings. A stroll around Brayford Pool also offers interesting insights into Lincoln's history, again flagged up by information boards that highlight the location's watery local and natural history.

Housed in a building dating from 1543, the Visitor Information Centre (see page 93) is an interesting sight in itself, and also provides maps for self-guided themed walks, though there is a small fee for these. Highlights of the Roman trail include vestiges such as **Newport Arch** (see page 51) and the **Well** at the corner of Westgate and Bailgate.

Beyond the city limits is the natural beauty of Lincolnshire's coast and countryside, where you can roam at will, and a number of further attractions that cost nothing beyond the small expense of getting there. The town of Sleaford offers a variety of free distractions, including the **National Centre for Craft & Design**, **Navigation House**, **Cogglesford Watermill** and **Cranwell Aviation Heritage Centre**. The RAF Digby **Sector Ops Museum** is also gratis, though donations are greatly welcome (see page 87).

When it rains

Anywhere in Britain, the chance of rain is high, particularly between October and March. Fortunately, most of Lincoln's major highlights – such as the cathedral, the Museum of Lincolnshire Life, the Usher Gallery and The Collection – are not only indoor attractions, but are all concentrated in the Uphill district. At the castle, the exhibition area in the former jail and vestiges of the castle's history are also under cover. (Leave the walk along the castle's ramparts for a cloudless day.)

In the Downhill district those who fancy a spot of shopping on a dismal day should make for the Waterside Centre and Central Market Halls, which offer an inviting and weatherproof retail environment. Visitors for whom shopping is less attractive may like to head to the Odeon cinema at Brayford Pool (see page 72) for a dry afternoon and the distraction of some big-screen entertainment. Another option is to head south away from the city centre, along the High Street to the historical, cultural and heritage centre inside **St Katherine's** (see page 73).

On arrival

ARRIVING
By air
Lincoln has no commercial airport of its own. However, three small airports lie reasonably close to the city (see page 90). Visitors touching down in the UK at one of London's airports should board a train to Lincoln from either London King's Cross or St Pancras International. The journey time is about two hours (see page 90).

By rail
One of the easiest ways of getting to Lincoln is by train. Although rail services are not as fast or as frequent as those serving other cities, travelling by train does mean that you will arrive right in the heart of the Downhill district. Taxis are available directly outside the station, as is the **Walk & Ride** bus service (see page 39), which provides a connection to the Uphill district.

By road
Lincoln is not particularly well served by major high-speed roads. Even once in the city, driving around can be somewhat problematic as its vast collection of historic, sometimes traffic prohibited streets can make navigation difficult. Drivers will find signs directing them around the city centre's outskirts that then offer spurs into the relevant areas (Cathedral Quarter and Cultural Quarter in the Uphill district and Brayford Pool and High Street in the Downhill district). It should also be noted

🔺 *Lincoln's railway station*

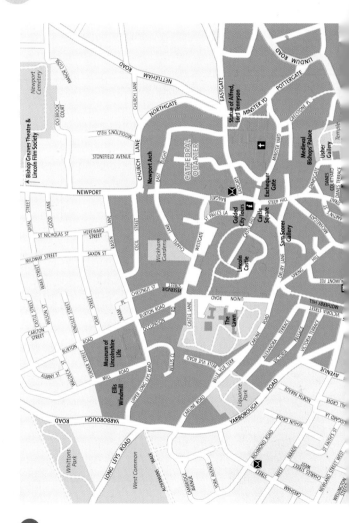

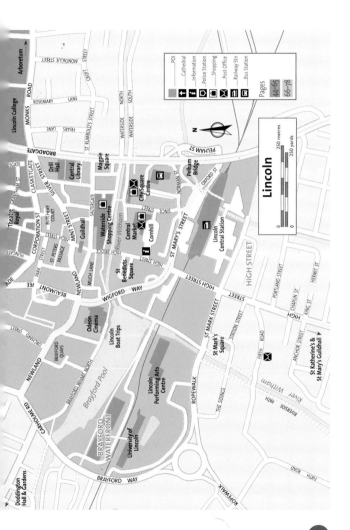

Lincoln

POI	
Cathedral	✚
Information	ℹ
Police Station	◉
Shopping	✕
Post Office	🏠
Railway Stn	🚂
Bus Station	R

Pages 44–65 66–78

N

0 — 250 metres
0 — 250 yards

that railway lines run through the Downhill area of the city, meaning that roads are often temporarily blocked at level crossings to let trains get through, which can cause added traffic congestion, particularly at peak times. Fortunately, across the whole of the city parking is quite plentiful, though all will require payment. In the Uphill area and from north to south, small car parks can be found on Westgate, Union Road, St Paul's Lane, Greetwellgate, Danesgate, Motherby Lane, Hungate and St Rumbold's Street. Downhill, there are larger car parks that tend to congregate around Brayford Pool and the university and which can be found on Lucy Tower Street, Broadgate, Wigford Way and among the St. Marks Shopping Centre. As yet there is no permanent **Park & Ride** scheme in Lincoln; however, during December's Christmas Market (see page 9), when many of the Uphill parking choices are closed off, a Park & Ride scheme is put in place using the Lincolnshire Showground on the A15 north of town. From here, visitors are transferred into the city by bus. Cost is on a per-car basis (around £10.00), paid on arrival.

FINDING YOUR FEET

Lincoln is a friendly city whose inhabitants are welcoming towards visitors. However, those who have yet to experience British bonhomie – boisterousness, particularly on weekend nights – may be a little taken aback. Also, although the British are normally overwhelmingly good natured, excessive alcohol intake can sometimes lead to rowdy behaviour in public. Should a crime take place or you strongly suspect one is about to, dial 999. For non-emergency calls contact the Lincolnshire

🔺 Buses need to be small on Lincoln's narrow streets

Constabulary (☎ 0300 111 0300). Not in any way connected to criminal elements, but like other large towns and cities in the UK, Lincoln has small numbers of homeless people who often sit in shop doorways asking for spare change, but they tend to be quiet and unassuming. Some homeless people are being helped to help themselves by selling a worthwhile national magazine called *The Big Issue*, which is always good for a browse over a coffee.

ORIENTATION

Lincoln can clearly be divided into two highly distinct areas: the Uphill and the Downhill districts. Both areas are largely pedestrian-friendly and relatively traffic-free. Most of the city's sights, independent shops and historic buildings are in the Uphill district, where the cathedral and the castle dominate the skyline. Within the Downhill district to the south are Brayford Pool, the university and the main retail and business area, concentrated along the High Street, the city's main artery.

Both the Uphill and the Downhill districts are quite compact. Walking from one to the other takes no more than 10 to 15 minutes, although the steep ascent to the Uphill district will certainly add some time and muscle tone. There are two gentler, albeit circuitous, ways of getting to the top of the Uphill district on foot. One involves walking westwards along The Avenue and Yarborough Road, and the other eastwards along Broadgate, Lindum Road and Pottergate. However, neither route is as visually rewarding as following The Strait and Steep Hill to the Uphill district.

GETTING AROUND

Lincoln's small size and predominantly traffic-free centre mean that the easiest way of getting around is on foot. However, those who prefer public transport, or who wish to avoid the steep walk to the top of the Uphill district, will find Lincoln's **Walk & Ride** buses a boon. Like the stops at which they call, the buses are easily identifiable by a large 'R' on their exterior. They provide a circular hop-on-hop-off service that connects the city's major sights, shopping areas, railway and bus station. They run every 20 minutes throughout the week (🕐 10.00–17.00 Mon–Sat, 12.00–17.00 Sun), and fares are around £1.30 for an adult single ticket and £3.00 for a day pass.

Destinations beyond the city limits are well served by a combination of train and bus. The city's main bus station (ⓐ Melville Street) is close to the railway station (ⓐ St Mary's Street) and travel information for both can be obtained from **Traveline** (🕿 0871 200 2233 🌐 www.travelineeastmidlands.co.uk). Alternatively, contact the Visitor Information Centre (see page 93). For those new to British bus transport, many buses are accessible for wheelchairs and child buggies. To catch a bus, first check that the routes at the stop correspond with the number at the front of the bus then raise an arm to signal to the driver that you want it to stop. Enter at the front and once on board give your destination to the driver (there are no conductors) and what sort of ticket you need (single, return, day pass, etc.). It's cash only and the correct change is generally appreciated, so carry some loose coins. A number of different bus companies operate in and out of the city and tickets are not necessarily transferable.

Cycling

The benefits of cycling for mind, body and planet are obvious, but Lincoln's hilly terrain means that only the extremely fit can get around everything that the city has to offer. The flat landscape surrounding the city, by contrast, was almost created for cycling and a series of trails along country lanes, old railway tracks and along riverbanks have been mapped and are supplied free of charge by Lincolnshire County Council (ⓦ http://microsites.lincolnshire.gov.uk/countryside) and from the Visitor Information Centre (see page 93).

Car hire

Hiring a car to get around Lincoln's compact centre is an unnecessary expense. However, if public transport is not practical, renting a car might be considered for reaching the surrounding suburbs, the Lincolnshire countryside or the coast. Costs and terms vary, but as a rough guide, a day's rental for a four-door medium-sized car should be in the region of between £40 and £50. In addition to a full driving licence, some car hire companies ask for two domestic utility bills as proof of address and identity.

▶ *The top end of Steep Hill*

THE CITY OF
Lincoln

Introduction to city areas

Although it is a relatively small city, in this guide Lincoln is
divided into two well-defined areas. This will help visitors
identify its sights and attractions and locate the best places
to eat and drink. On the map the delineation is very
straightforward and in the city itself this will become even more
apparent. Taking Corporation Street, Clasketgate and Monks
Road as one continuous boundary, City North, better known as
the Uphill district, is the hillside and hill top portion of the city.
This is the location of the bulk of the city's distinctive historic
and cultural riches alongside some fine eateries and shops.
Getting to the Uphill district on foot is a breathtaking
experience in every sense. South of this line, City South, or the
Downhill district, extends into the city's suburbs and a small
collection of surrounding attractions. The flat terrain here
includes Brayford Pool, the main university campus and Lincoln's
principal retail, commercial and business area. This is also where
visitors arriving by public transport will first set foot on
Lincoln soil.

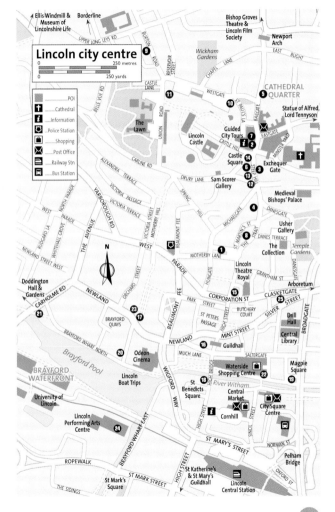

Lincoln city centre

0 ———————— 250 metres
0 ———————— 250 yards

POI
Cathedral
Information
Police Station
Shopping
Post Office
Railway Stn
Bus Station

City North, the Uphill district

Clearly the primary area of interest for visitors, this enchanting medieval district is packed with spectacular history stretching back 2,000 years, as well as some fine hotels and many charming shops and cafés. This historic heart is still a residential area, and this, together with its elevated hilltop setting, gives it a separate village-like feel, quite distinct from the more modern city directly below. The Visitor Information Centre (see page 93) is situated here, as is a small post office (ⓐ Bailgate ⓑ 09.00–17.30 Mon–Fri, 09.00–17.00 Sat).

SIGHTS & ATTRACTIONS

Arboretum
Restored to its former glory, this public park is a relaxing place to spend some downtime. Created by the celebrated Victorian gardener Edward Milner, it has green spaces, fountains and water features, a children's play area and a maze all linked by a lovely and broad tree-lined avenue. The Arboretum also commands fine views of the city. ⓐ Monks Road ⓑ 07.00–22.00 daily

Ellis Windmill
This windmill, to which entry is free, is the last surviving one out of the original sixteen that once crowded the city's hilltop. Now fully restored, it offers visitors a working insight (subject to favourably windy conditions) into the production of flour. It is close to the Museum of Lincolnshire Life, under whose custodianship it exists. ⓐ Mill Road ⓣ 01522 528448

ⓦ www.lincolnshire.gov.uk/visiting/museums ⓛ 14.00–17.00
Sat & Sun (Apr–Sept); 14.00–dusk Sun (Oct–Apr) ⓝ Bus: Walk &
Ride (see page 39) ⓘ Given its structural design, the building is
only partially accessible to those with limited mobility

Exchequer Gate

This magnificent 14th-century ceremonial gateway leads to the
cathedral. It is thought that its passages, topped by former
apartments, may once have formed part of a medieval shopping

▲ *Ellis Windmill*

centre, where shops were incorporated into the building surrounding the square (including the 13th-century Church of St Mary Magdalene). Exchequer Gate is also said to have been the place where tenants paid their rents to church landlords, whose practice of laying out a chequered cloth on which to count out the coins was the origin of the name 'exchequer'.

ⓐ Castle Square

The Lawn

Another of Lincoln's free hidden gems is The Lawn, located in a tranquil expanse of green beneath the castle's western walls. At its heart is a former hospital complex built in 1820 where resident doctors who had once provided therapy to George III continued their pioneering work on the treatment of mental illness. Long since closed, the buildings now house a number of attractions but the main draw for visitors is the Sir Joseph Banks Tropical Conservatory (ⓣ 01522 568080 ⓛ 10.00–17.00 Mon–Sat, 10.30–17.00 Sun). One of Lincolnshire's most famous sons, Joseph Banks was the chief scientific officer on Captain Cook's expedition of 1768 aboard the *Endeavour*, and he was also responsible for establishing the Royal Botanic Gardens at Kew.

Passing through the gift shop, the walk around the intimate tropical house traces Banks's botanical journey around the southern hemisphere. Also contained within The Lawn complex is the small John Dawber walled gardens (ⓛ 08.00–17.00 daily (summer); 08.00–16.00 daily (winter)). There are also water features, beds dedicated to oriental plants and a sensory area.

ⓐ Union Road

Lincoln Castle

This is one of the most splendid and best-preserved Norman castles in Britain. Walk through its imposing gates and you are off on a 900-year journey back in time. Its solid ramparts and intriguing towers command views across the city and surrounding countryside that are worth the entrance fee in themselves. However, it is the original Victorian and Georgian

◯ *The castle ramparts*

TIME TRAVELLERS PASS

This three-day discount ticket can be used to make savings on entry to the castle, cathedral and Medieval Bishops' Palace. An individual pass and family pass (for two adults and three children aged between 5 and 16) is available, and it can be purchased either online (🅦 www.visitlincolnshire. com) or at the Visitor Information Centre (see page 93). Some restrictions apply during certain events in the city.

prison buildings within that contain the castle's star attractions. These include the cells, chapel, first-hand accounts and collections of artefacts that provide a haunting reminder of what life, justice and punishment were like in the 19th century.

Given this heritage of crime, it is apt that the castle is also home to one of only four copies of Magna Carta. Proclaimed in 1215, this 3,500-word 'Great Charter' laid down the foundations of basic laws still applied today in the UK and the rest of the democratised world, and was central to sowing the seeds of civil liberty. Also here is the lesser-known but unique Charter of the Forest, a slightly later and nationally important proclamation that guaranteed the rights of 'common folk' to work and to roam common land without fear of punishment. ⓐ Castle Hill ❶ 01522 511068 🅦 www.lincolnshire.gov.uk/lincolncastle ⓛ 10.00–18.00 daily (May–Aug); 10.00–17.00 daily (Apr & Sept); 10.00–16.00 daily (Oct–Mar) (last admission 45 minutes before closing) ⓝ Bus: Walk & Ride (see page 39) ❶ Admission charge. Some events, such as the Christmas Market, prevent access to the prison and exhibition rooms

Lincoln Cathedral

Towering above the city and the surrounding countryside, this is one of Europe's most spectacular dedications to Christianity. A soaring place of worship for the past millennium and a marvel of engineering skill and artisanship, this cathedral is a must on any itinerary around Lincoln.

The original cathedral was completed around 1092, though most of the building collapsed during a rare and violent earthquake in 1185. Only the glorious west front and its main

🔺 *Lincoln Cathedral by night*

entrance were left standing. The rest of the present building dates from the 12th to the 14th centuries. It contains many exquisite features, such as the Dean's Eye and Bishop's Eye in the rose windows, and woodcarvings in the Angel Choir and St Hugh's Choir. More latterly, the cathedral was used by the Germans as a vital landmark for bombing raids during World War II, and as such it was never targeted by the Luftwaffe. The building was also used as a film location for *The Da Vinci Code* and *Young Victoria*, standing in as a substitute for Westminster Abbey.

The twice-daily general guided tours are free with entry tickets (🕐 Variable, according to season). They are coupled with other specific tours (including a visit to the rooftop), which need to be booked in advance from the information centre within. If bored children or adults are in tow, challenge them to search out the famous Lincoln Imp to help keep them amused (see box, page 54). On a bright day, try to visit in the morning, when sunlight streams through the south-facing stained-glass windows to create colourful shapes on the floor and wall opposite. Mornings are also the time when the building is at its most tranquil. By contrast, evensong (🕐 17.30 daily) and the cathedral's busy schedule of recitals offer a wonderful chance to experience the building's sensational acoustics and atmosphere. 🅐 Minster Yard 🕿 01522 561600 🌐 www.lincolncathedral.com 🄴 visitors@lincolncathedral.com 🕐 07.15–20.00 Mon–Fri, 07.15–18.00 Sat & Sun (summer); 07.15–18.00 Mon–Sat, 07.15–17.00 Sun (winter) (hours may change to accommodate certain events) 🅝 Bus: Walk & Ride (see page 39) 🅘 Admission charge

Lincoln Guided Tours

Starting from the Visitor Information Centre (see page 93), these 90-minute walking tours around Lincoln's historic gems reveal the city's interesting facts and quirky anecdotes. The walks are led by qualified guides and are offered in several languages. ⓐ Castle Square ⓣ 01522 521256 ⓦ www.lincolnguidedtours. co.uk ⓛ 11.00 daily (July & Aug) (check in advance for other days as these vary depending on the season) ⓘ Guide charge; advance booking is not required

Newport Arch

Built during the 3rd century, this is one of the finest of Lincoln's Roman remains. Uniquely in Britain, traffic is still allowed to

◆ The 3rd-century Newport Arch

pass beneath it. The pedestrian gate attached to it is a medieval addition and the whole structure was originally much taller than it is now, having slowly disappeared beneath layers of subsequent development. An information board tells the full tale of Newport Arch, including the episode of how a truck once got stuck driving through it. ⓐ Bailgate

Statue of Alfred, Lord Tennyson

At the grand age of 81 and charging only for materials, the celebrated English artist G F Watts sculpted this splendid figure of his close friend with his pet Russian wolfhound. Tennyson (1809–92), a son of Lincolnshire, was made poet laureate in 1850. 'The Charge of the Light Brigade' was just one of many poems that made him so popular during the Victorian era, and led to his being buried in Westminster Abbey. Today it's not uncommon for pranksters to pop a traffic cone on top of the statue's head. ⓐ Cathedral Gardens

Steep Hill & The Strait

As well as being the nucleus of Lincoln's big-hitting attractions, this is also home to one of the finest collections of medieval buildings in the UK. As its apt name suggests, Steep Hill (leading on to The Strait) is best explored on foot, and it's not easy at that, but the effort is worth it and, for a well-earnt sit down, the considerate burghers of Lincoln recently installed some benches at Steep Hill's junction with Danesgate.

There are plenty of charming and historic buildings to admire along the way. Most house alluring shops, cafés or restaurants, but it's always worth looking above the modern

shop frontages to get a glimpse of the original architecture
(see page 58). Highlights include the 12th-century **Norman
House** (ⓐ 47 Steep Hill) and the slightly older **Jew's House**
(ⓐ 15 The Strait; see page 63) which is thought to be the oldest
secular residential building in Britain. The neighbouring Jew's
Court stands on the site of a medieval synagogue, though it
dates back only 300 years, close to the time when, in this street,
house numbers were used as part of an address for the very first
time in Britain.

CULTURE

Bishop Greaves Theatre

Also known as the BG theatre, this intimate venue located in the
city's northern suburbs stages lesser-known, more considered
touring productions (some created for children) along with
weekly film screenings (see page 54). ⓐ Bishop Grosseteste
University College, Longdales Road ⓣ 01522 583761 ⓦ www.
bishopg.ac.uk

The Collection

Next door to the Usher Gallery, this modern family-friendly
museum, which has free entry, takes visitors on a journey
through the ancient and natural history of the local area. The
museum, which is not intimidatingly large, has a wealth of
ancient and prehistoric archaeology on display, with lots of
interactive fun to keep both children and adults engaged.
There is also a café. ⓐ Danes Terrace ⓣ 01522 550990
ⓦ www.thecollection.lincoln.museum ⓛ 10.00–15.45 daily

Lincoln Film Society

The society holds weekly screenings of the best in world and independent cinema not usually found in the large multiplexes. Membership is required, though a limited number of day passes are available before each show. Enquire in advance for details. ❷ Bishop Greaves Theatre, Longdales Road ❶ 01522 583761 Ⓦ www.lincolnfilm.org.uk 🕒 19.30 Fri

Lincoln Theatre Royal

Charming, intimate and rich in neo-rococo colour and detail, this recently restored Victorian theatre hosts a formidable programme of touring and repertory productions that range from rock tribute

---

THE LINCOLN IMP

According to a 14th-century legend, the Lincoln Imp was dispatched by the Devil to cause as much mischievous mayhem as possible inside Lincoln Cathedral. An angel was sent to halt the damage but the imp continued to hurl things around from a safe height. Having failed to reason with it, the angel finally resorted to turning the grinning demon to stone. This tale of the triumph of good over evil is the most popular explanation of how the imp came to be set in stone. This iconic symbol of the city is just 30 cm (12 in) tall, and spotting it in the cathedral's interior can be quite a challenge. Those who prefer to seek it for themselves should read no further: it's over the last complete column on the left of the Angel Choir.

acts and classic and contemporary musicals through to opera, ballet, Shakespearean plays and weighty dramas. ➌ Clasketgate ☏ 01522 519999 ⓦ www.lincolntheatreroyal.com ⏰ Box office: 10.00–18.00 Mon–Sat, 13.00–18.00 Sun (until 19.30 on show days)

Medieval Bishops' Palace

Overlooked by the cathedral, yet often bypassed by visitors, this palace was the nerve centre of the largest and most powerful diocese in England. Even what remains of the building today gives a clue as to the wealth and power of the Church in the Middle Ages. First constructed in the 12th century, it played host to a number of visiting kings and queens (including Catherine Howard, fifth wife of Henry VIII) before it was finally ransacked during the English Civil War. The palace is now but a shadow of its former opulent self, but an audio-tour offers an insight into daily life and work here, in what was once one of the country's most important buildings.

There are some great views from the lower terrace (also a good place for a picnic) and a small vineyard (yes, in Lincoln!) to explore for those who don't want to attempt the spiral staircase climb up Alnwick Tower. ➌ Minster Yard ☏ 01522 527468 ⓦ www.english-heritage.org.uk ⏰ 10.00–17.00 daily (summer); 10.00–16.00 Thur–Mon (winter) (last admission 45 minutes before closing) Ⓝ Bus: Walk & Ride (see page 39) ❶ Admission charge. The palace is on a slope with steps to negotiate

Museum of Lincolnshire Life

Created from the remnants of a former army barracks that once housed the Royal Lincolnshire Regiment, this charming and intriguing museum, with free entry, explores and re-creates the domestic, agricultural, industrial and military lives of Lincolnshire people over the past 300 years. The region has long been associated with agriculture. However, Lincoln itself also has a long and illustrious history of engineering, with tank manufacturing a particular speciality. On display here is the locally made Flirt II, an original battle tank that saw action on the Western Front during World War I. Very much a Lincoln invention, these 'land ships' created by local engineers William Foster and Co. were to change the course of warfare forever. It is worth taking time to watch the audiovisual presentation to get a fuller account of this imposing machine.

Children are kept entertained by a series of tasks during their tour. There is also a small, inexpensive café. The museum is a gentle ten-minute amble on the flat from the sights of Castle Square. ⓐ Burton Road ⓣ 01522 528448 ⓦ www.lincolnshire. gov.uk/visiting/museums ⓛ 10.00–15.30 daily (Apr–Sept); 10.00–15.30 Mon–Sat (Oct–Mar) ⓝ Bus: Walk & Ride (see page 39)

Sam Scorer Gallery

This small gallery is run by a trust dedicated to promoting works of art in differing media by new and established local artists. The works are displayed for two weeks at a time, in a rolling programme of exhibitions. ⓐ 5 Drury Lane ⓣ 01522 589899 ⓦ www.samscorergallery.co.uk ⓛ 10.00–16.00 Tues–Sun

Usher Gallery

Traditional and modern art, furniture, ceramics and a rich collection of clocks fill the rooms of the Usher Gallery, another of Lincoln's free cultural attractions. This two-floor gallery not only houses permanent works by such luminaries as J M W Turner, L S Lowry, Patrick Caulfield and Grayson Perry, but also dedicates space to a programme of prestigious touring exhibitions loaned from such institutions as London's Tate Gallery and National Portrait Gallery. Its modest size means that interest should not flag. Also look out for pieces of sculpture in the surrounding gardens. ⓐ Danes Terrace ⓣ 01522 550990 ⓦ www.thecollection. lincoln.museum ⓒ 10.00–15.45 daily

△ *Usher Gallery*

RETAIL THERAPY

Those never happier than when ambling from one unique shop
to another will certainly find Lincoln's Uphill district an absolute
joy. There are so many retail gems here that a separate guide
would be needed to cover them all. Everything from retro
clothing to independent butchers, from dealers in the
antiquarian to chocolatiers and from whisky specialists to high-
end designer fashion can be found along these sometimes
precipitous cobbled streets. Castle Square, the castle courtyard,
Steep Hill and The Strait are also areas that are taken over by
the city's famous Christmas Market and its series of regular
specialist markets with their appealing stalls.

TAKING A BREAK

CAFÉS

The Cheese Society £ ❶ A hugely popular café and specialist
cheese shop, this bright and breezy small eatery serves a selection
of lighter snacks such as croque-monsieur and grilled rarebit along
with more substantial dishes such as steak and risotto. Wines and
beers are sold to accompany the fine food on offer. ⓐ 1 St Martin's
Lane, off Hungate ❶ 01522 511003 ⓦ www.thecheesesociety.co.uk
🕐 10.00–16.30 Mon–Sat (last food order 15.30), closed Sun
❶ Children under ten not allowed; reservations not taken so it is
worth arriving early or later in the afternoon

The Ice Cream Parlour £ ❷ Established in 1926, this ice-cream
parlour uses milk and cream from its nearby farm to create over

30 delicious additive-free treats. These can be enjoyed in the historic ambience of an oak-panelled room or the vaulted cellar of a former inn. ⓐ 3 Bailgate ⓣ 01522 511447 ⓦ www.dennetts.co.uk ⓛ 11.00–17.30 daily

Lesley's On The Hill £ ❸ One of many helping to maintain the traditions and etiquette of high tea, this tea room offers a choice of savoury bites and sugary indulgences served on china and silver by cheerful ladies in traditional uniforms. ⓐ 39 Steep Hill ⓣ 01522 522463 ⓛ 07.45–18.00 Mon–Fri, 09.00–18.00 Sat, 10.00–17.00 Sun

⬢ The Whisky Shop in Lincoln's Uphill district

Pimento Cafe £ ❹ Hidden at the back of a groovy fashion and accessory shop, this excellent and very informal vegetarian and vegan bistro is full of enticing and creative dishes, and has a good choice of teas and coffees. It offers a welcome break from Lincoln's hill-climbing exertions. ⓐ 26A Steep Hill ❶ 01522 544880 ❶ 10.00–17.00 Mon–Sat, 10.30–17.00 Sun

RESTAURANTS

Thailand No.1 £ ❺ This endearing and extremely well-liked Thai restaurant serves all the expected favourites as well as a selection of lesser-known authentic offerings that are either à la carte or part of a choice of set meals. Staff are charming and the setting lovely, particularly in the conservatory

● *The traditional bar of The Victoria*

during the summer. **ⓐ** 80–81 Bailgate **ⓣ** 01522 537000
ⓦ http://lincoln.thailandnumber1.co.uk **ⓛ** 12.00–14.30, 18.00–
23.00 Mon–Sat, 18.00–22.30 Sun

Brown's Pie Shop ££ ⓺ A multi-award-winning establishment
and a firm favourite, this intimate, friendly eatery specialises in
historic pies and local signature dishes such as the legendary
Lincolnshire sausage and red beefsteak. The small cellar is
especially charming and romantic, its allure enhanced by the
knowledge that T E Lawrence (Lawrence of Arabia) lodged here
while serving in the RAF. **ⓐ** 33 Steep Hill **ⓣ** 01522 527 330
ⓦ www.brownspieshop.co.uk **ⓛ** 12.00–14.30, 17.00–21.30 Mon–
Sat, 12.00–20.00 Sun

Gino's ££ ⓻ Almost a victim of its own success, the popularity
of this busy trattoria-style Italian joint was helped along by its
owner, who starred in the television documentary *Dolce Vito*,
which filmed his efforts to open a British restaurant in Italy. All
the firm pasta and pizza favourites are here, along with a solid
à la carte menu and affordable wine list. Especially busy at
weekends. **ⓐ** 7 Gordon Road, off Bailgate **ⓣ** 01522 513770
ⓦ www.ginoslincoln.co.uk **ⓛ** 12.00–14.00, 18.00–22.00 daily

The Jews House Restaurant ££ ⓼ Housed in one of the city's
most celebrated and historic buildings (see page 53), and
recently re-opened after a devastating fire, this restaurant offers
fine dining in every sense. Dishes are inspired by British and
European cuisine, and the carefully considered menu is a
celebration of local produce combined with imagination,

presented with flair and served with aplomb. @ 15 The Strait
☎ 01522 524851 **ⓦ** www.jewshouserestaurant.co.uk **🕒** 12.00–
14.00, 19.00–21.00 Tues–Sat, closed Sun & Mon

The Old Bakery £££ ❾ A ten-minute walk from the cathedral,
along an unremarkable suburban street, leads to an
extraordinary restaurant bristling with awards and personal
accolades. The style of the interior is simple chic, but the food is
an inspirational journey both round the world and through the
creative imaginations of some serious culinary talent. Local
produce is heavily championed, with à la carte and tasting
menus, and guest bedrooms. @ 26–28 Burton Road **☎** 01522
576057 **ⓦ** www.theold-bakery.co.uk **🕒** 12.00–14.00, 19.00–21.00
Tues–Sat (last order for taster menu 19.30), 12.00–14.00 Sun

BARS & PUBS
Cloud Bar £ ❿ Rare for this area of the city, this is a swish and
modern bar and restaurant serving a mixed menu of
established pub favourites, pies, burgers, curries and the like
alongside a selection of tapas dishes. For an especially arresting
sight at sunset, head upstairs to the rooftop terrace and sip a
cocktail against the backdrop of some marvellous views over
the floodlit castle and cathedral. Drink and meal deals are
available, as is free Wi-Fi. @ 1 St Paul's Lane **☎** 01522 511284
ⓦ www.thecloudbar.co.uk **🕒** 11.00–23.00 Mon–Thur, 10.00–
01.00 Fri–Sun

The Victoria £ ⓫ A little off the visitor radar, this small
traditional pub next to the castle's western gateway is a must

for those who like their hostelries simple and unpretentious yet crowded with ephemera. Simple yet hearty food is on offer, and outside there is a large partially covered space for alfresco refreshment. **ⓐ** 6 Union Road **ⓣ** 01522 541000 (ext 4) **ⓦ** www. victoriapub. net **ⓛ** 11.00–24.00 Mon–Thur, 11.00–01.00 Fri & Sat, 12.00–24.00 Sun

Widow Cullen's Well £ ⓬ One of the best places in Lincoln for a beverage and a winning combination of old and new, this pub offers two floors of distraction-free conviviality and drinking. There is no jukebox, fruit machine or karaoke, just a good selection of affordable real ales and lovely places to sit and enjoy the surroundings. Food is also served, though this

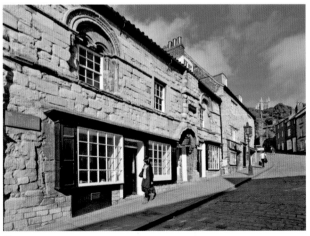

◣ *The Jews House Restaurant*

is not really what this place is about. A visit to the lavatory is a must to discover how the pub got its name. ⓐ 29 Steep Hill ⓣ 01522 523020 ⓛ 12.00–23.00 Mon–Sat, 12.00–22.30 Sun ⓘ There is wheelchair access at the rear

Wig & Mitre £ ⑬ Downstairs is a small convivial pub while upstairs, with its oak beams and Victoriana, is the dining room – a slightly more formal setting for a mosaic of dishes from around the world. Reflecting the chef's dedication to seasonal produce, the menus change every 12 weeks and gourmet evenings are regularly held to promote the best in fresh ingredients. ⓐ 32 Steep Hill ⓣ 01522 535190 ⓦ www.wigand mitre.com ⓛ 09.00–22.00 daily (food), 08.30–23.00 daily (bar)

△ *Ghost walks leave from Castle Square*

AFTER DARK

Several fine traditional pubs are to be found in Lincoln's Uphill district (see pages 61–2). While some stay open to around midnight and offer small-scale live entertainment, this is not the area for late revelry among pounding beats and disco balls. Anyone in search of a place to dance the night away or to see some of the big-name acts that happen to be in town should make their way to the Downhill district.

City Ghost Walks ⑭ One of Lincoln's most popular attractions, these walking tours of terror reveal chilling tales of the macabre and strange paranormal goings-on in the shadows of streetlights and in moonlit medieval buildings and alleyways. The walks last for around 90 minutes each and are suitable for families. There is no need to book in advance but you should arrive 10 minutes early. ⓐ Visitor Information Centre, 9 Castle Hill ⓣ 01522 874056 ⓦ www.lincolnhistorywalks.co.uk ⓛ 19.00 Wed–Sat ⓘ Tour charge

Sakura ⑮ Stylish Japanese-themed nightclub popular with students during the early part of the week, when prices for entry and drinks plummet. The rest of the week Sakura caters to the city's sophisticates. ⓐ 280–281 High Street ⓣ 01522 525828 ⓦ www.sakuralincoln.com ⓛ 10.00–03.00 Mon & Wed–Sat, 11.00–03.30 Tues, closed Sun

City South, the Downhill district

While very much the business end of Lincoln and lacking much of the historic charm and magnetism of the Uphill district, the Downhill area has its rewards, especially for those hell-bent on shopping at the familiar big-name high-street retail outlets. This is certainly also *the* place to head for for late-night partying. Yet Downhill has another, more tranquil face: several waterside sights here are certainly worth a little time. This is also the area where the main university campus is laid out and where Lincoln's newer chain hotels have sprung up.

SIGHTS & ATTRACTIONS

Brayford Pool

Often considered the reason why a settlement was established here, this expanse of water has been used as an inland harbour for thousands of years. It was made navigable for shipping by the Romans, thus connecting Lincoln to river networks and international trade and setting the course for the city's expansion and prosperity. But the coming of the railways in the 19th century put paid to Lincoln's waterborne trading.

Today, Brayford Pool is a popular leisure marina and nightlife spot, with bars and restaurants along the north bank. There are a number of information boards along its waterside, which is the departure point for cruises along the Fossdyke (see opposite). ⓐ Brayford Wharf North and East ⓦ www.lincoln city.co.uk ⓝ Bus: Walk & Ride (see page 39)

Lincoln Boat Trips

A gentle cruise westwards along the Fossdyke, dug by the Romans, takes you out of the city, through the suburbs and into the Lincolnshire countryside. The 50–60-minute cruise aboard the *Brayford Belle* offers a choice of heated indoor or outdoor seating and a café, all complemented by a commentary. This is also the place for private motorboat hire, with prices ranging from £15 to £20 an hour. ⓐ Brayford Wharf North ⓣ 01522 881200 ⓦ www.lincolnboattrips.com ⓛ 11.00–15.45 daily (Easter–Sept); Sat & Sun (Oct) (five departures) ⓝ Bus: Walk & Ride (see page 39) ⓘ Ticket charge and a minimum of four passengers needed for each cruise to depart

ⓐ *Boat trips start at Brayford Pool*

River Witham

Running through the city, this narrow canal cut by the Romans stretches for 58 km (36 miles) to Boston, in southeast Lincolnshire. The canal side through the city centre is a

● *The Empowerment Statue traverses the River Witham*

delightful spot: City Square is a good place to take a seat, feed the ducks and swans and admire the colourful narrowboat traffic passing by. An unmissable landmark here is Stephen Broadbent's dramatic **Empowerment Statue**, which spans this historic watery byway. Standing 16 m (52 ft) high, it is a steel and aluminium turbine blade that celebrates Lincoln's engineering past. ➌ City Square

St Mary's Guildhall

This historic building, a little way out of the city centre, is said to have been built for ceremonial purposes by Henry II. It has since served as a royal wine store, a guildhall and a malting house, as well as shops and storage sheds. It now houses the Lincoln Civic Trust. Within the building is a visible stretch of the Fosse Way, a major Roman road, complete with ruts made by the wheels of horse-drawn vehicles. ➋ 385 High Street ☎ 01522 546422 ✉ lincolncivictrust@btinternet.com 🕓 By prior arrangement

THE GLORY HOLE

The space beneath the medieval arches of High Bridge has for centuries been known as the 'Glory Hole', an eyebrow-raising term used by boaters to reflect its dimensions for waterway traffic passing through on the River Witham. 'Glory Hole' is also the name of the alleyway that runs alongside the waterway towards Brayford Pool. When first built, it was called the 'Murder Hole', because dead bodies thrown into the river washed up here.

CULTURE

Doddington Hall & Gardens

Owned by the same family since it was completed in 1600, this grand home retains all its original external features, including its façade, walled courtyards and award-winning gardens. Inside, however, the fixtures and furnishings have moved with the times, though they still offer a wonderfully engaging tale of domestic life over the past 400 years. A full day could be spent wandering through the house with the character-led audio-tour, then sauntering in the extensive grounds. There are activities for children, a great café and one of the best farm shops in the area. Although the house is 8 km (5 miles) from the city centre, it's

⏷ The handsome façade of Doddington Hall

well worth making the effort to get here, despite the lack of public transport (taxis are a good alternative). ⓐ Doddington ⓣ 01522 694308 ⓦ www.doddingtonhall.com ⓛ House (13.00–17.00) and gardens (11.00–17.00) Wed, Sun & Bank Holiday Mon (Easter–Sept); gardens only 11.00–16.00 Sun (Feb, Mar & Oct) ⓘ Admission charge

Drill Hall

Another of the city's busy performance venues, this former military and police training hall now presents a rich mixture of theatre, stand-up comedy and concerts of all musical genres alongside family shows and daytime lectures. ⓐ Free School Lane, off Silver Street ⓣ 01522 873894 ⓦ www.lincolndrillhall.com ⓛ Box office: 10.00–17.00 Mon–Sat, closed Sun ⓝ Bus: Walk & Ride (see page 39)

Guildhall

This gateway, which stands on the site of the south entrance to Roman Lincoln, dates from 1520. The official home of the city's mayor, the building houses a large number of fine civic objects, including a sword donated by Richard II, Charles I's mace of office and the city's charter of 1157, which predates Magna Carta. The building also contains the former debtors' prison and a 14th-century bell, which is still rung. Guided tours are available and private visits can be arranged by appointment, but if you can't get inside the building the stone carvings on its southern façade are certainly worth a look. ⓐ Corner of Stonebow and High Street ⓣ 01522 541727 ⓦ www.lincolnshire.gov.uk ⓛ 10.30, 13.30 Fri & Sat

Lincoln Performing Arts Centre

This modern theatre (known as LPAC) within the university campus hosts an impressively eclectic programme of drama, family shows, dance, comedy and classical music. ⓐ University of Lincoln, Brayford Wharf East ⓣ 01522 837600 ⓦ www.lpac.co.uk ⓛ Box office: Shared with The Engine Shed (see page 78) ⓐ Bus: Walk & Ride (see page 39)

Odeon Cinema

Nine screens of big-film entertainment in the heart of the city alongside a collection of waterfront bars and restaurants.

🔺 *The state-of-the-art LPAC theatre*

ⓐ Brayford Wharf North ☏ 0871 224 4007 ⓦ www.odeon.co.uk
ⓝ Bus: Walk & Ride (see page 39)

St Katherine's

At the southern end of the High Street and a 25-minute
walk from the Downhill district, this newly refurbished church
is now a heritage and cultural centre. Displays trace the history
of this 900-year-old site. There are interactive features for
children as well as a continual programme of special events.
ⓐ St Katherine's ☏ 01522 572778 ⓦ www.stkatherineslincoln.
co.uk ⏲ 10.00–16.00 Tues–Sat ⓝ Bus: 1, 13, 14

RETAIL THERAPY

The hub of Lincoln's shopping opportunities, the pedestrian-
friendly stretch of the High Street is lined with such well-known
shops and department stores as **House of Fraser**, **Marks &
Spencer**, **Boots** and **WH Smith**. Further south, where traffic joins
the street, there is little of merit. Also on the High Street is the
enclosed comfort of the Waterside Centre (☏ 01522 529566
ⓦ www.watersideshopping.com) while parallel to it on Sincil
Street are **Cornhill** and **Central Market Halls** (ⓦ www.
lincolnmarket.co.uk). Next to these is Cornhill, the outdoor
location of some of the city's farmers' and craft markets (see
page 14).

St Mark's Shopping Centre, a little further south, has major
stores such as **Tesco**, **Debenhams** and **BHS Home** as well as
various fast-food outlets (ⓐ St Mark's Square ☏ 01522 575240
ⓦ www.stmarks-lincoln.co.uk). For some truly independent local

produce, **The Farmers' Market** is held in Cornhill (2nd Thur of the month), while further afield, the **Doddington Farm Shop** (see page 70) trade in some truly wonderful food, some of which comes with almost zero food mileage.

◐ *The Barge on the Brayford*

TAKING A BREAK

CAFÉS

Coffee Aroma £ **⑯** Exceedingly good ethically sourced coffee conjured up by friendly people who know their way around a Barista. Food is served through the day and a small collection of artworks and a book exchange upstairs all add to the magnetism of this fashionable coffee bar. **❸** 5 Guildhall Street, off High Street **ⓦ** www.coffeearoma.co.uk **ⓔ** info@coffeearoma.co.uk **ⓛ** 08.00–17.30 Mon–Thur, 08.00–20.00 Fri & Sat, 10.30–16.30 Sun

Fodders £ **⑰** This small, low-key deli has an extremely high reputation. It is an excellent spot to grab a picnic and head to nearby Brayford Pool to watch aquatic birdlife and waterway traffic. **❸** 27 Newland **ⓣ** 01522 567311 **ⓛ** 07.30–14.30 Mon–Fri

Stokes High Bridge Cafe £ **⑱** The Stokes family have been trading in tea and coffee since 1902, but the history of this place goes much further back. Dating from the 16th century, it perches on top of the 12th-century High Bridge (see box, page 69), which is said to be the oldest bridge in the UK still to bear buildings. The café is split into three compact levels, and the first- and second-floor windows provide views of the river-patrolling swans below. The cheerful staff serve up light bites, substantial meals and some excellent cakes, as well as hot drinks and food to go. **❸** High Bridge, High Street **ⓣ** 01522 513825 **ⓦ** www.stokes-coffee.co.uk **ⓛ** 08.00–16.30 Mon–Sat, 11.00–16.30 Sun **ⓛ** Limited access upstairs

RESTAURANTS, BARS & PUBS

The Green Dragon £ ⑲ This 16th-century half-timbered tavern is on the banks of the River Witham. The interior is divided into two. The larger ground floor area is a comfortable eating space where hefty international favourites are on the menu. Downstairs is an intimate cellar where beer lovers can enjoy a broad choice of real ales. The small terrace outside offers views of the river, but the sound of busy traffic from the adjoining road can make conversation difficult. ⓐ Broadgate ⓣ 01522 567155 ⓦ www.greendragonpub.co.uk ⓛ 11.00–24.00 Mon–Sat, 12.00–22.30 Sun

Prezzo £ ⑳ A relatively inexpensive place to eat, this large Italian restaurant and bar oozes modern style and sophistication among the creams and browns of its furnishings, setting it apart from the other bars and restaurants along the Brayford waterfront. It is part of a large chain of restaurants known for inhabiting interesting buildings. The semicircular bar offers lovely views across the marina, especially at night, while the menu delivers all the pizza and pasta staples alongside a choice from the grill. ⓐ The Glassmill, Brayford Wharf North ⓣ 01522 528595 ⓦ www.prezzorestaurants.co.uk ⓛ 12.00–23.30 daily

The Barge on the Brayford ££ ㉑ Along the waterfront of Brayford Pool is a choice of large and modern places to eat and drink, but what sets this small, genial place apart from the rest is the fact that it occupies a still-floating, 80-year-old wheat and corn boat called *Prudence*. The galley signature dishes are predominantly based on fish and seafood, though offerings grown and reared from the land are also available. Lighter snacks are served at lunchtime and there is an open deck for clement weather. ⓐ Brayford Wharf North ⓣ 01522 511448 ⓦ www.bargeonthebrayford.com ⓛ 11.30–21.00 Mon–Fri, 11.30–22.00 Sat, 11.30–20.00 Sun

Kashi ££ ㉒ Informal and friendly canteen-style Japanese sashimi and sushi house on the banks of the River Witham. Everything is prepared fresh to order from the open kitchen and the extensive choices come with tasting menus to help ease the choice and cost. ⓐ 22 Waterside North ⓣ 01522 521444 ⓦ www.kashijapaneserestaurant.co.uk ⓛ 12.00–15.00, 17.30–23.00 Mon–Sat, 12.00–22.00 Sun

SONS & DAUGHTERS

A fertile ground for talent, Lincolnshire claims many famous sons and daughters, including the poet Alfred, Lord Tennyson; Elton John's songwriter Bernie Taupin; Colin Dexter, creator of Inspector Morse; the actresses Dame Sybil Thorndike, Dame Joan Plowright, Patricia Hodge, Lynda Bellingham and Jennifer Saunders; the adventurer Captain John Smith, of Pocahontas fame; former prime minister Margaret Thatcher; and the scientist Sir Isaac Newton. Less well known is Chad Varah, who was responsible for the formation of the Samaritans.

AFTER DARK

CLUBS & VENUES

Christopher's ㉓ One of the few, if not the only, dedicated gay bars in the city. Regular cabaret helps the fun along with a number of theme nights. ⓐ 35 Newland ❶ 01522 567329 ⓦ www.christopherslincoln.com ⓛ 20.00–late Tues–Sun

The Engine Shed ㉔ A nightclub, a bar and the city's largest gig venue for touring bands and comedians. The Tower bar is a popular hangout for students and those wanting to watch live sports on TV. ⓐ University of Lincoln, Brayford Wharf East ❶ 0844 888 8766 ⓦ www.engineshed.co.uk ⓛ Box office: 12.00–14.00 daily (summer); 10.00–16.00 Mon–Fri (winter) ❶ ID for proof of age required

Pulse, Ritzy & JJ's ㉕ Three dance clubs in one offer a broad spectrum of popular tunes to help cut some shapes and witness some occasional live gigs. Rarely cool, but a popular destination at weekends. ⓐ 11 Silver Street ❶ 01522 522314 ⓦ www.pulselincoln.co.uk ⓛ 22.00–03.00 Tues, Wed, Fri & Sat, 22.30–03.00 Thur, 23.00–03.00 Sun

▶ *Chocolate-box scenes in the Lincolnshire Wolds*

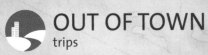
OUT OF TOWN
trips

Lincolnshire Wolds

A bucolic expanse of chequered hues dappled with red-roofed cottages beneath huge skies, the Lincolnshire Wolds are an Area of outstanding natural beauty but are often unjustly overlooked. The gently undulating pastoral landscape is perfect for some easy walking and cycling along ancient tracks that link historic and handsome market towns. The Blue Stone Heath Road between Welton le Wold and Calceby is an especially gratifying route. This is also the location of some of the county's famous aviation sites (ⓦ www.visitlincolnshire.com).

GETTING THERE

This broad area has a good choice of bus services connecting Lincoln with the main towns of Alford, Horncastle, Louth, Market Rasen and Woodhall Spa. By car, follow the A158 east then the A157 to the heart of the Wolds.

SIGHTS & ATTRACTIONS

Alford Windmill

Perhaps the finest working example of a flour mill in the UK, the windmill is open for tours. There is also a shop selling flour ground here and a café. ⓐ East Street, Alford ⓣ 01507 462136 ⓦ www.alford-windmill.co.uk ⓛ 10.00–17.00 Tues–Sat, 11.00–17.00 Sun (July–Sept); 10.00–17.00 Tues, Fri & Sat, 11.00–17.00 Sun (Apr–June & Oct); 10.00–16.00 Tues & Sat, 11.00–16.00 Sun (Nov–Mar)

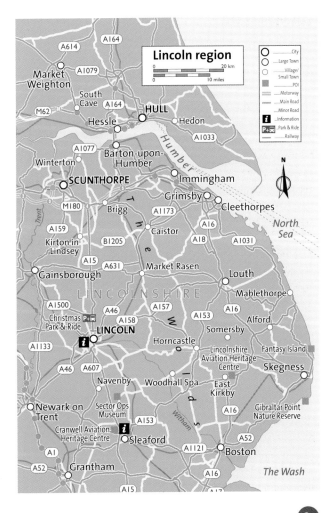

Kinema in the Woods

Offering a joyous film-going experience of yesteryear, this restored 90-year-old cinema presents a bill of contemporary and classic films. It even has a working organ. Going to multiplexes will never be the same again. ⓐ Coronation Road, Woodhall Spa ① 01526 352166 ⓦ www.thekinemainthewoods. co.uk ① Showing times vary, so contact in advance

Lincolnshire Aviation Heritage Centre

This former Bomber Command airfield features an evocative collection of buildings, transport and artefacts. Star of the show is its Avro Lancaster, which can be ridden down the taxiway. ⓐ East Kirkby, near Spilsby ① 01790 763207 ⓦ www.lincsaviation.co.uk ① 10.00–16.00 Mon–Sat (summer); 10.00–15.00 Mon–Sat (winter) ① Admission charge. Advance bookings only for the Avro Lancaster ride

Somersby

The village is a place of pilgrimage for lovers of the poet Alfred, Lord Tennyson, who was born in the rectory (now a private house) and whose father was a clergyman at Somersby's 15th-century church. The summit of Warden Hill offers commanding views of the village and the surrounding area.

RETAIL THERAPY

Though it is not strictly in the Wolds, Hemswell is only a short journey away. It is worth a visit for the antiques and collectables at the mammoth **Hemswell Antiques Centre** (ⓐ Hemswell Cliff,

Gainsborough ☎ 01427 668389 ⓦ www.hemswell-antiques.com
🕐 10.00–17.00 daily). The town of Horncastle is also well regarded
in the antiques trade, while Louth has a good choice of
independent retailers.

TAKING A BREAK

Myers Bakery & Café £ This is the place to get afternoon tea or
to enjoy a lunch of well-made sandwiches, omelettes and
salads. Their shop is next door should you prefer a picnic.
ⓐ 20 The Bullring, Horncastle ☎ 01507 525453
ⓦ www.myersbakery.co.uk 🕐 09.00–16.00 daily

Melanies ££ Lovely and highly commended restaurant that takes
its food quality and sourcing extremely seriously. The menu is
classic British, with creative European twists. ⓐ 37 Upgate, Louth
☎ 01507 609595 ⓦ www.melaniesoflouth.com 🕐 12.00–14.00,
18.30–21.00 Wed & Thur, 12.00–14.00, 19.00–22.00 Fri, 19.00–
22.00 Sat, 12.30–14.30 Sun ❶ Advance booking recommended

🔺 *The gloriously quirky Kinema in the Woods*

Skegness

Quite an assault on the senses, this Lincolnshire-style Las Vegas is a brash yet endearing seaside resort that certainly splits opinion. Set in an ocean of static caravans, for many this is a fantastically fun place to come for a sensory barrage of garish entertainment, bright lights, big sounds and coronary-inducing food. For everyone else these are the reasons for not coming. Whichever side you fall on, there is no denying that there are plenty of thrills and spills. The beach and promenade gardens are pleasant and the young at heart should have a ball.

GETTING THERE

From Lincoln you can reach Skegness either directly by bus (ⓝ Bus: 6) or by train. By car, simply follow the A158.

SIGHTS & ATTRACTIONS

Fantasy Island
From extreme thrills to gentle children's rides, this enormous theme park, 5 km (3 miles) north of Skegness, has a theatre and a large choice of bars, food stalls, shops and market. ⓐ Sea Lane, Ingoldmells ⓣ 01754 615860 ⓦ www.fantasyisland.co.uk ⓛ Rides 10.30–22.00 daily (Easter–Nov) ⓝ Bus: 1 (Skegness bus station)

Gibraltar Point Nature Reserve
An antidote to brash Skegness, the dunes, marshes and lagoons of this 5-km (3-mile) length of unspoilt coastline are a renowned

habitat for an array of bird species. There is also a visitor centre, café and small gift shop. ⓐ Gibraltar Road ⓣ 01754 898057 ⓦ www.lincstrust.org.uk ⓛ Visitor centre and café 10.00–16.00 daily (summer); 11.00–15.00 daily (winter)

Natureland Seal Sanctuary

Primarily a place for the study and rehabilitation of seals, this fun, family-friendly centre also houses penguins, tropical fish, birds and reptiles. Feeding times are twice a day. ⓐ North Parade ⓣ 01754 764345 ⓦ www.skegnessnatureland.co.uk ⓛ 10.00–16.30 daily (summer); 10.00–15.00 daily (winter) ⓘ Admission charge

RETAIL THERAPY

Although Skegness boasts Europe's largest outdoor market (see Fantasy Island, opposite) and Hildreds Shopping Centre (ⓐ Briar Way), it is fair to say that only those who are looking for novelty trinkets and cigarette lighters sold by the bag will find much reward in Skegness.

TAKING A BREAK

A wealth of takeaway places cluster around Tower Esplanade, while cafés and bars line Grand Parade.

The Royal Hotel £ Just a short walk from the town, this is both a British/American restaurant (ⓛ 12.00–14.30, 19.30–21.30 daily) and an Indian restaurant (ⓛ 17.00–23.30 daily). ⓐ South Parade ⓣ 01754 762301 ⓦ www.theroyalhotelskegness.co.uk

Sleaford

The bustling market town of Sleaford has a long history,
highlighted by such features as the 13th-century Church of
St Denys, and a 17th-century school and almshouses. The
picturesque tree-lined banks of the River Slea offer the
opportunity for a pleasant stroll. Surrounding the town are
just some of Lincolnshire's famous aviation attractions
(ⓦ www.visitlincolnshire.com).

GETTING THERE

Lying 31 km (19 miles) south of Lincoln, Sleaford is easy to reach
by train (the town centre is a five-minute walk from the station)
or by bus (Ⓑ Bus: 31). By car, take the A15 south.

SIGHTS & ATTRACTIONS

Cogglesford Watermill
A short, pleasant walk from the town centre, this scenic working
mill grinds out organic flour. ⓐ East Road ⓣ 01529 413671
ⓦ www.heartoflincs.com ⓛ 12.00–16.00 Mon–Fri, 11.00–16.30
Sat & Sun (Apr–Oct)

Cranwell Aviation Heritage Centre
Artefacts and interactive exhibits help tell the story of nearby
RAF Cranwell, the first military air academy in the world.
ⓐ North Rauceby ⓣ 01529 488490 ⓦ www.heartoflincs.com
ⓛ 10.00–16.30 daily (Apr–Oct); 10.00–16.00 Sat & Sun (Nov–Mar)

The Hub

This former seed store now houses the National Centre for Craft & Design. It has three galleries, workshops, children's activities, a shop and a café. From the upper floors there are good views of the red-roofed town. ⓐ Navigation Wharf ⓘ 01529 308710 ⓦ www.thehubcentre.info ⓛ 10.00–17.00 daily

Mrs Smith's Cottage

Built in the 19th century and little changed since the 1920s, this humble cottage offers a fascinating insight into local domestic life. ⓐ 3 East Road, Navenby ⓘ 01529 488490 ⓦ www.mrssmithscottage.co.uk ⓛ 13.00–16.00 Wed–Sun (Aug); 13.00–16.00 Fri–Sun (June, July & Sept); 13.00–16.00 Sun (Mar–May & Oct–Nov) ⓘ Admission charge

Navigation House

Located beside The Hub (see above), these canal offices of 1838 have been converted into a heritage centre that charts the life and times of the Sleaford Navigation, the impact it had on the town and future plans to reopen it. ⓐ Navigation Wharf ⓘ 01529 308102 ⓦ www.heartoflincs.com ⓛ 12.00–16.00 Mon–Fri, 11.00–16.30 Sat & Sun (Easter–Sept); 12.00–16.00 Sat & Sun (Oct–Easter)

Sector Ops Museum

A still operational airbase offering a 90-minute guided tour around its restored Fighter Command Operations Room. The tour highlights the airbase's vital role in Britain's

wartime defence. ⓐ Ashby de la Launde ⓣ 01526 327619
ⓦ www.raf.mod.uk/rafdigby ⓛ 11.00 Sun (May–Oct)

RETAIL THERAPY

Although it is a pretty little town, Sleaford is not particularly
good for shopping. However, market days (Mon, Fri & Sat) bring
some colour and life, and there is a diverting gift shop at The
Hub (see page 87).

TAKING A BREAK

Curio Cafe £ A towering beacon in the heart of Sleaford, this
converted windmill offers seasonal local salads, sandwiches and
cakes in unique surroundings. ⓐ Money's Yard, Carre Street
ⓣ 01529 309990 ⓦ www.moneyscafe.co.uk ⓛ 10.00–15.00
Mon–Sat

Cogglesford Mill Cottage Restaurant ££ In a riverside setting
just out of town, this place is great for sampling Lincolnshire
produce (some from the restaurant's own garden), prepared
with skill and panache. ⓐ East Road ⓣ 01529 309409
ⓦ www.cogglesfordmillcottage.co.uk ⓛ 10.30–16.30 Tues & Sun,
10.30–16.30, 18.30–21.00 Wed–Sat (Easter–Oct); 11.00–16.00 Tues
& Sun, 11.00–16.00, 18.30–21.00 Wed–Sat (Nov–Easter)

▶ *Clear signposting near Newport Arch*

PRACTICAL
information

Directory

GETTING THERE

By air

Three airports are local to Lincoln. The nearest is Robin Hood Airport (☎ 0871 220 2210 ⓦ www.robinhoodairport.com), which is 45 minutes from the city by car. Humberside Airport (☎ 0844 887 7747 ⓦ www.humbersideairport.com) is 50 minutes from Lincoln by car, while East Midlands Airport (☎ 0871 919 9000 ⓦ www.eastmidlandsairport.com) is 90 minutes away.

Many people are aware that air travel emits CO_2, which contributes to climate change. You may be interested in the possibility of lessening the environmental impact of your flight through the charity **Climate Care** (ⓦ www.jpmorgan climatecare.com), which offsets your CO_2 by funding environmental projects around the world.

By rail

Lincoln is not best served by direct rail services from major cities. There are some services from London Kings Cross, with a change at Newark (Northgate), Retford, Peterborough or Doncaster. For details contact **National Rail** (☎ 0845 748 4950 ⓦ www.nationalrail.co.uk).

By road

Unusually for a city, Lincoln has no motorway link. The nearest major trunk route is the A1; approaching from the south, drivers should branch off on to the A15 or A46, and from the north the

A57. **National Express Coaches** has daily services from London's Victoria Coach Station (☎ 0871 781 8178 ⓦ www.national express.com).

Cycle hire
Barnes Cycles (ⓐ 85 Newport ☎ 01522 519813) has a limited number of bicycles for hire in the city centre. Students who sign up to the 'cycLIN' scheme can hire bikes during term time (☎ 01522 837874 ⓦ www.sustrans.org.uk (see page 40)).

Taxis
Lincoln's licensed cabs sport a licence plate inside and out and can be either hailed in the street or booked in advance. There is a taxi rank outside the railway station and on Newland. Privately run minicabs must be booked in advance.
Discount Cabs ☎ 01522 800800 ⓦ www.discountcabs.co.uk
Lincoln Taxis ☎ 01522 899899 ⓦ www.lincolntaxicabs.co.uk

HEALTH, SAFETY & CRIME
Crime in Lincoln is well below the national average. However, as in all places that attract visitors, Lincoln is not immune to the attentions of thieves who prey on the unprepared and distracted. Basic precautions include keeping cash and valuables close to your body and hidden away. When using an ATM, shield the keyboard from potential prying eyes. Before going out be sure to carry your hotel's business card in case you get lost. Importantly, never let companions go wandering off alone if they've had too much to drink. Finally, for first-time visitors to Britain, the tap water is safe to drink.

MEDICAL SERVICES

If you need to consult a doctor, ask for help at your hotel reception or call **NHS Direct** on ☎ 0845 4647 (🌐 www.nhsdirect. nhs.uk).

Emergency dental treatment is available at Lincoln Dental Care (📧 472 Newark Road ☎ 01522 682030 🕐 08.00–20.00 Mon–Fri, 09.00–16.30 Sat, 09.00–12.30 Sun).

The central **NHS Walk-In Centre** also offers treatment and assessment for more minor illnesses and injuries (📧 63 Monks Road ☎ 01522 528153 🕐 08.00–20.00 daily (closed Easter Sunday & Christmas Day)).

Late-night pharmacy Boots 📧 The Carlton Centre, Outer Circle Road ☎ 01522 511890 🕐 08.30–24.00 Mon–Wed, 08.00–24.00 Thur–Sat, 10.30–16.30 Sun

Lincoln County Hospital has more comprehensive facilities, as well as an A&E unit (📧 Greetwell Road ☎ 01522 512512 🌐 www.ulh.nhs.uk 🚌 Bus: 4, 15, 15A).

OPENING HOURS

Most shops and attractions open from 09.00 or 10.00 to 17.30, Monday to Saturday, and from 11.00 to 16.00 on Sundays and bank holidays. Banks are open from 09.30 to 17.00 Monday to Friday, and on Saturday mornings.

TOILETS

Public lavatories are situated in the following locations: Westgate Car Park, The Lawn, Castle Street Car Park, Silver Street, The Waterside Centre, the bus station and the railway station.

CHILDREN

Many of the attractions that feature in this guide make efforts
to entertain and interest children, but to help children let off
some steam head to play areas of the Arboretum, Hartsholme
Country Park and Whisby Nature Park (see pages 20–21). The
resort of Skegness is another obvious alternative.

TRAVELLERS WITH DISABILITIES

Lincoln opens itself up to disabled visitors as much as possible.
However, its ancient buildings and steep streets, some of which
are cobbled, can make access and mobility a challenge (see
page 39). **Shopmobility** offers rental equipment including
wheelchairs and scooters. (ⓐ Lincoln Area Dial-a-Ride &
Shopmobility, Bus Station, Melville Street ⓣ 01522 514477
ⓦ www.shopmobilityuk.org ⓛ 09.00–12.00, 13.00–16.30 Mon–
Sat ⓘ Hire fee and reservation required; restrictions apply).

FURTHER INFORMATION

Visitor Information Centre ⓐ 9 Castle Hill ⓣ 01522 545458
ⓦ www.visitlincolnshire.com ⓔ visitorinformation@
lincolnbig.co.uk ⓛ 10.30–16.00 Mon–Sat, 10.30–15.00
Sun (summer); 11.00–15.00 Mon–Sat (winter) (closed Sun,
New Year's Day, Christmas Day & Boxing Day)

Other useful websites include:
ⓦ www.heritageconnectlincoln.com
ⓦ www.lovelincoln.co.uk
ⓦ www.thelinc.co.uk
ⓦ www.thisislincolnshire.co.uk

A

accommodation 22–5
airports 32, 90
Alford Windmill 80
Alfred, Lord Tennyson statue 52
annual events 8–9
antiques and collectables 82–3
Arboretum 20, 44
art galleries 27, 30, 56–7
arts see culture
attractions
City North (Uphill district) 44–53
City South (Downhill district) 66–9
free 30
Lincolnshire Wolds 80, 82
Skegness 84–5
Sleaford 86–8
top 26–7
wet weather 31

B

Bailhouse Hotel 24
banks 92
Barge on the Brayford 76–7
bars and pubs 62–3, 65, 76, 78
begging 38
Bishop Greaves Theatre 53
Blue Stone Heath Road 80
boat trips 67
Brayford Pool 30, 66
British Summer Time 8
Brown's Pie Shop 61
buses 32, 39–40

C

cafés 58–60, 75, 83, 88
camping and caravanning 25
canal 68–9
car hire 40
cathedral and churches 6, 26, 46, 49–50, 73
Charlotte House 23–4
Cheese Society, The 58
children 93
Christmas Market 9, 14–15, 26
cinema 19, 54, 72–3, 82

city areas
City North 6, 31, 38, 42, 44–65
City South 6, 31, 38, 42, 66–78
City North (Uphill district) 6, 31, 38, 42, 44–65
City South (Downhill district) 6, 31, 38, 42, 66–78
climate 8
Climate Care 32, 90
Cloud Bar 62
clubs 65, 78
coach services 91
coastline 20, 84–5
Coffee Aroma 75
Cogglesford Mill Cottage Restaurant 88
Cogglesford Watermill 86
Collection, The 26, 30, 53
comedy events and venues 9, 71, 72
concerts 71, 72
craft fair 14
Cranwell Aviation Heritage Centre 86
crime 38, 91
Crown Windmill 24–5
culture 12
City North (Uphill district) 53–7
City South (Downhill district) 70–73
Curio Café 88
cycle hire 91
cycling 20, 40

D

dental treatment 92
directory 90–93
disabilities, travellers with 93
discount tickets 48
Doddington Hall and Gardens 70–71
Downhill district see City South
Drill Hall 71
drinking water 91
driving 32, 36, 40, 90–91

E

eating and drinking 16
City North (Uphill district) 58–64
City South (Downhill district) 75–7
Lincolnshire Wolds 83
Skegness 85
Sleaford 88
Ellis Windmill 44–5
Empowerment Statue 69
entertainment 18–19
see also nightlife
Exchequer Gate 45–6

F

famous Lincoln citizens 77
Fantasy Island 84
farmers' markets 14, 74
festivals 8–9
Fodders 75
food specialities 16
football 20
Fosse Way 69
free attractions 30

G

gay and lesbian life 9, 78
ghost walks 26, 65
Gibraltar Point Nature Reserve 84–5
Gino's 61
Glory Hole 69
golf 20
Green Dragon 76
guesthouses 24
Guildhall 71

H

Hartsholme Country Park 20–21, 25
Hemswell 82–3
High Bridge 69, 75
history 10–11
Holiday Inn 22
Horncastle 83
horse racing 20
hospital 92
hotels 22–4
Hub, The 87

I

Ibis Hotel 22
Ice Cream Parlour, The 58–9

itineraries 28–9

J
Jew's House 53
Jews House Restaurant 61–2
John Dawber walled gardens 46

K
Kashi 77
Kinema in the Woods 82

L
Lawn, The 46
Lesley's On The Hill 59
Lincoln Castle 26, 31, 47–8
Lincoln Cathedral 6, 26, 49–50
Lincoln Film Society 54
Lincoln Guided Tours 51
Lincoln Holiday Homes 25
Lincoln Hotel 23
Lincoln Imp 54
Lincoln Performing Arts Centre 72
Lincoln Theatre Royal 54–5
Lincolnshire Aviation Heritage Centre 82
Lincolnshire Wolds 20, 27, 80, 82–3
Louth 83

M
Magna Carta 48
maps 34–5, 43, 81
symbols 4
markets 14
medical services 92
Medieval Bishops' Palace 55
Melanies 83
motorboat hire 67
Mrs Smith's Cottage 87
Museum of Lincolnshire Life 27, 30, 55–6
museums 26, 27, 30, 53, 55–6, 82, 86, 87–8
Myers Bakery & Café 83

N
National Centre for Craft & Design 87
nature reserves 21, 84–5
Natureland Seal Sanctuary 85

Navigation House 87
Newport Arch 51–2
nightlife 18
City North (Uphill district) 65
City South (Downhill district) 78
Norman House 53

O
Old Bakery, The 24, 62
Old Rectory, The 24
opening hours 92
orientation 38–9
out of town
Lincolnshire Wolds 20, 27, 80, 82–3
Skegness 84–5
Sleaford 30, 86–8

P
parking 36
parks and gardens 20–21, 44, 46, 70–71
pharmacy, late-night 92
picnics 16
Pimento Café 60
police 38
Prezzo 76
prices 4

R
restaurants 60–62, 76–7, 83, 85, 88
River Witham 68–9
road, arriving by 32, 36, 90–91
Robin Hood 18
Roman remains 30, 51–2
Royal Hotel 85

S
safety 38, 91
St Katherine's 73
St Mary Magdalene Church 46
St Mary's Guildhall 69
Sam Scorer Gallery 56
seasons 8
Sector Ops Museum 87–8
self-catering 24–5
Shopmobility 93
shopping 14–15, 58, 73–4, 82–3, 85, 88, 92

Sir Joseph Banks Tropical Conservatory 46
Skegness 27, 84–5
Sleaford 30, 86–8
Somersby 82
sport and relaxation 20–21
Steep Hill 52–3
Stokes High Bridge Cafe 75
Strait, The 52–3
street performers 19

T
taxis 32, 91
Temple Gardens 20
Tennyson, Alfred, Lord 52, 82
Thailand No.1 60–61
theatre 19, 53, 54–5, 71, 72
theme park 84
Time Travellers Pass 48
toilets 92
tourist information 30, 93
trains 32, 90
travel
to Lincoln 32, 36, 90–91
within Lincoln 36, 39–40, 91

U
Uphill district see City North
Usher Gallery 27, 30, 56–7

V
Victoria, The 62–3
Viking street names 11
vineyard 55
Visitor Information Centre 30, 93

W
Walk & Ride bus service 32, 39
walking 20, 30, 38–9
walking tours 51
walks, self-guided 30
Warden Hill 82
Washingborough Hall 23
wet-weather attractions 31
Whisby Nature Park 21
White Hart Hotel 23
Widow Cullen's Well 63–4
Wig & Mitre 64
Willow Holt 25

ACKNOWLEDGEMENTS
The photographs in this book were taken by Paul Walters for Thomas Cook Publishing, to whom the copyright belongs.

Project editor: Thomas Willsher
Copy editor: Lucilla Watson
Layout: Paul Queripel
Proofreaders: Karolin Thomas & Ceinwen Sinclair
Indexer: Marie Lorimer

AUTHOR BIOGRAPHY
David Cawley is an author, travel writer and occasional broadcaster. A member of the British Guild of Travel Writers and published throughout the world, he specialises in British city breaks and history.

Send your thoughts to
books@thomascook.com

- Found a great bar, club, shop or must-see sight that we don't feature?
- Like to tip us off about any information that needs a little updating?
- Want to tell us what you love about this handy little guidebook and more importantly how we can make it even handier?

Then here's your chance to tell all! Send us ideas, discoveries and recommendations today and then look out for your valuable input in the next edition of this title.

Email the above address (stating the title) or write to:
pocket guides Series Editor, Thomas Cook Publishing, PO Box 227, Coningsby Road, Peterborough PE3 8SB, UK.